Properties of Matter

by Ann J. Jacobs

What is matter?

Everything is made of matter.
Matter is anything that takes up space
and has mass.

Mass is how much matter is in something.
All things made of matter have mass.
Everything you see is made of matter.

Matter is made of small parts.
A hand lens helps you see small parts
up close.
Some things you cannot see are made
of matter.
Air has matter!

Properties of Matter

Different kinds of matter have different properties.

A **property** is something you can observe about an object.

Color is a property of matter.
Shape is a property of matter.
Size is a property of matter too.

What colors are the pipe cleaners? Are they big or small?

How much something weighs is a property of matter.

How something feels is a property of matter.

Do you think the sponge weighs a lot?

Is the brush hard or soft? How does the cup feel?

What are the states of matter?

There are three **states of matter.**
The states of matter are solids, liquids, and gases.

Gas

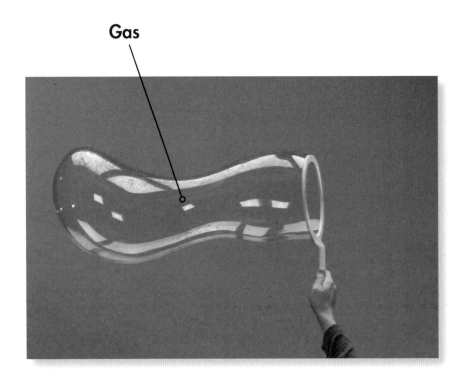

Solid

Liquid

A **solid** is matter that has its own size and shape.
Solids take up space.
Solids have mass.

Use a ruler to find out how long, wide, and tall solids are.

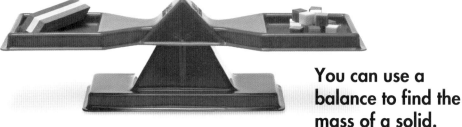

You can use a balance to find the mass of a solid.

Crayons are solids.
Each crayon has a color.

Notebooks are solids.
Notebooks have a shape.

Liquids

Liquid is matter that does not have its own shape.
Liquids take the shape of what they are in.
Liquids take up space and have mass.

Water is a liquid.

Put water in a jar.

The water will take the shape of the jar.

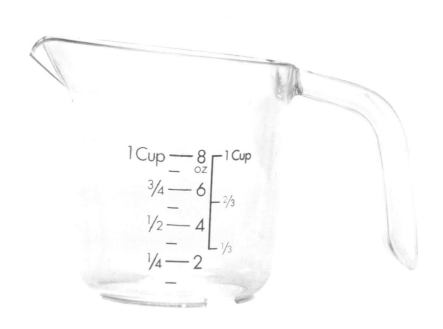

**Liquids can be measured.
Use a cup such as this one.
Volume is the amount of
space a liquid takes up.**

Gases

Gas does not have its own shape.
Gas is matter that takes the size and shape of what it is in.
Gas takes up all the space inside what it is in.

Gas fills the balloons. Gas takes the size and shape of the balloons.

Gas can change size and shape.
Gas has mass.
You breathe air.
Air is made of gases.

Gas fills the bubble. Gas takes the size and shape of the bubble.

How can matter be changed?

Matter can be changed in many ways.
You can change the size of matter.
You can change the shape of matter.

**Fold paper into
a new shape.**

**Press clay into
a new shape.**

Rip paper to
change its size.

Bend a pipe cleaner
to change its shape.

Mixing and Separating Matter

You can put different kinds of matter together.
This makes a mixture.

A **mixture** is made up of two or more
things.
These things do not change.

This is a mixture of fruits.
You can see each part.
You can separate a mixture.
The parts stay the same.

Mixing with Water

Some mixtures are made with water.
This mixture is made with sand and water.

Look at this mixture. You can see the sand and the water.

This mixture is made with salt and water.
There are different ways to separate
mixtures.
The matter can sink.
The water can evaporate.

Look at this mixture. What do you think will happen when the water evaporates?

How can cooling and heating change matter?

Water is matter.

Water can change.

Water will freeze when it is very cold.

You can freeze liquid water to make ice.

The water will change to ice.
Ice is solid water.

Rain will freeze when it is
cold. Water on the leaves
changed from a liquid to
a solid.

Water as a gas is water
vapor. It changes to a liquid
when it meets a cold glass.
See the water drops.

Heating Matter

Heating can change the state of matter.
Heat can change solids to liquids.
Heat can change liquids to gases.

Ice and snow melt when it is warm.
Solid water changes to a liquid.

Heat from the Sun makes water evaporate.

Heat can change other matter from
solids to liquids.
Butter melts when you heat it.

Look at the matter around you.
What will stay the same?
What can change?

Glossary

gas   matter that has mass and can change size and shape

liquid   matter that takes up space and has mass, but does not have its own shape

mass   the amount of matter in an object

mixture   something made up of two or more things that do not change

property   something about an object that you can find out with your senses

solid   matter that has its own mass, shape, and size

states of matter   solids, liquids, and gases